MAY – 3 2017

Dorothea Lange

The Photographer Who Found the Faces of the Depression

CAROLE BOSTON WEATHERFORD   pictures by SARAH GREEN

ALBERT WHITMAN & COMPANY
CHICAGO, ILLINOIS

*B*ecause childhood polio left her with a limp and a rolling gait, Dorothea knew how those less fortunate felt without ever walking in their shoes.
Kids called her "Limpy."

After her parents split, school-age Dorothea
donned a cloak of invisibility to pass the vagabonds
in New York's Bowery neighborhood on walks home alone.
Years later, she could walk without fear
among demonstrating dockworkers
to document their bloody strike.

Dorothea realized she had "eyesight"
but was a so-so student who skipped school,
didn't like being told what to do, and barely graduated.
She said that she aimed to be a photographer.

After teacher-training school and working part-time
in a fashionable Fifth Avenue portrait studio,
Dorothea went cross-country with her friend Fronsie.
They got robbed in San Francisco
and Dorothea wound up working
at a department store's photo-finishing counter.
Within months, she opened her own studio.

To break with her past, strong-willed Dorothea
took her mother's maiden name—
Lange—and donned bold silver jewelry,
a jaunty black beret, and flowing skirts to hide her limp.
Her studio was an after-work hangout
where Bohemians drank tea and danced to jazz.

Dorothea married Maynard Dixon,
a dashing artist who wore cowboy boots.
But the marriage was doomed by money troubles
and his long painting trips that left her at home,
juggling photography with housework and childcare.

When her son gave her daisies for Mother's Day,
Dorothea photographed the bouquet.

Dorothea also tried nature photography.
While paused during a thunderstorm on a solo hike,
she had an awakening that brought her purpose into focus.
She was meant to photograph people—
not just the wealthy but from all walks of life.

Dorothea stepped behind the camera
and out into the world.
On San Francisco's Skid Row,
she photographed men
sleeping on sidewalks,
leaning against storefronts,
and a man slumped beside
an overturned wheelbarrow.

Economics professor Paul Taylor was drawn
to Dorothea's street photos in an Oakland gallery
and invited her to illustrate an article of his.
Before long, she joined him in his fieldwork.
Dorothea took pictures of Paul's interview subjects.
The two were kindred spirits and eventually married.

Dorothea was moved by the life histories
uncovered by Paul's team of researchers.
She began jotting down quotes and field notes
and pairing her images and captions in photo essays.
More than a photographer, she was a storyteller with a camera.

The government soon hired her as a field investigator.
With a bulky box camera, Dorothea hit the road
to show America to Americans. What others neglected
or ignored, she noticed and preserved on film:
an ex-slave in Alabama, sharecroppers
in the South, migrant workers out West,
rural poverty programs, and later during World War II,
Japanese Americans in internment camps.

Dorothea's subjects were scattered in different regions.
She sometimes drove hundreds of miles a day,
going slow to study the scenery.
At each stop, she climbed onto her car's roof
and surveyed the surroundings.

One day, through driving rain, she spotted
a sign for a migrant camp. Although ending
a month-long assignment and yearning for home,
Dorothea drove into the wet and soggy camp and parked.

Rains had destroyed the pea crop, and with it, hopes for work. Laborers were breaking camp and leaving, but Dorothea approached a family that was staying put. For days, they had eaten only wild birds and frozen vegetables from the fields and had sold their car's tires to buy food. Dust storms had driven them out of Oklahoma to the West to work as farm laborers.

Now the family was stranded and starving.
Dorothea shot a half-dozen or so pictures
of the mother and her children—
the last a close-up of the woman's deeply lined face.
She looks much older than her thirty-two years.

After two of the photos ran in the newspaper,
the government rushed ten tons of food to the camp.

Because Dorothea turned her lens on hunger and poverty,
Florence Owens Thompson, a full-blooded Cherokee,
became the face of the Great Depression.
And the nation could not look the other way.

ABOUT DOROTHEA LANGE

Dorothea Lange was one of the leading documentary photographers of the twentieth century. Her photographs focused national attention on poverty and injustice.

Born in 1895 in Hoboken, New Jersey, Dorothea was one of two children born to Heinrich and Johanna Nutzhorn. At age seven, Dorothea was stricken with polio. The illness left her with a limp but also with compassion for the less fortunate.

Her father abandoned the family when Dorothea was twelve. Angry, she eventually took her mother's maiden name, Lange. After her mother got a job as a librarian on New York's Lower East Side, Dorothea attended school in the city.

She was a mediocre student but had a keen eye. After high school graduation she planned to enter the male-dominated field of photography. To please her mother, though, she attended a teacher's college. At the same time, Dorothea studied photography at Columbia University and apprenticed with Arnold Genthe, a famed New York portrait photographer.

In 1918 Dorothea set off with a friend to tour the world. The trip abruptly ended when their wallets were stolen in San Francisco. Dorothea got a job at a department store as a photo finisher. Soon she opened her own portrait studio where she hosted after-work gatherings of creative types like artist Maynard Dixon, whom she married in 1920.

Maynard's extended painting trips left Dorothea to run the household and to raise his daughter and their two sons. She found it difficult to juggle her career and motherhood. For a while she and Maynard lived in separate studios and paid someone to board their children, as cash-strapped families sometimes did then.

During the Depression, Dorothea trained her lens on the jobless, hungry masses. In a local gallery, her photographs caught the eye of economics professor Paul Taylor. He invited Dorothea to join him in the field. The two eventually divorced their spouses and married.

The couple documented hardships in rural America for the Farm Security Administration and the Resettlement Administration. Dorothea began taking her own field notes.

In 1936 at a migrant labor camp in Nipomo, California, she photographed thirty-two-year-old Florence Owens Thompson, whose family was starving.

Among the photos was the iconic image *Migrant Mother*. After a newspaper published the photo, the government rushed aid to the camp.

In 1940 Dorothea became the first woman awarded a coveted Guggenheim Fellowship. During World War II, the Office of War Information hired her to photograph the forced evacuation and incarceration of Japanese Americans. In 1945 Dorothea documented the San Francisco conference that created the United Nations. That same year, she joined the faculty of the California School of Fine Arts. Despite poor health, she took assignments from *Life* magazine and cofounded *Aperture*, a magazine and book publisher devoted to photography. Dorothea also continued to travel with her husband—and her camera—to Asia, South America, and elsewhere, documenting the world.

Dorothea Lange died in 1965 and was inducted into the International Photography Hall of Fame and Museum in 1984.

Photos from left to right: *Migrant Mother*, February 1936; *Dorothea Lange, Resettlement Administration photographer, in California*, February 1936; *Striking longshoremen during the waterfront strike in San Francisco, California*, March 1937

For all who dare to see—CBW

**To my parents and family for supporting my goals.
Your encouragement has meant the world to me.—SG**

Library of Congress Cataloging-in-Publication data is on file with the publisher.

Text copyright © 2017 by Carole Boston Weatherford
Pictures copyright © 2017 by Sarah Green
Photographs by Dorothea Lange, Library of Congress, Print & Photographs Division,
LC-DIG-fsa-8b29516 and LC-DIG-fsa-8b31724
Published in 2017 by Albert Whitman & Company
ISBN 978-0-8075-1699-7

Printed in China
10 9 8 7 6 5 4 3 2 1 LP 20 19 18 17 16

Design by Jordan Kost

For more information about Albert Whitman & Company,
visit our web site at www.albertwhitman.com.